W9-CGV-149

Everything You Need To Know About

DRUG ABUSE

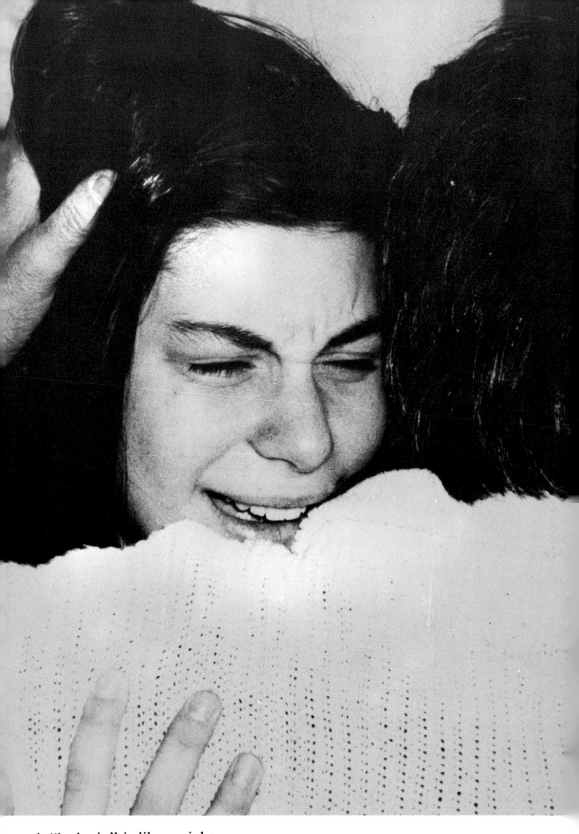

A "bad trip" is like a nightmare.

• THE NEED TO KNOW LIBRARY •

Everything You Need To Know About

DRUG ABUSE

Jacqueline A. Ball

Series Editor: Evan Stark, Ph.D.

THE ROSEN PUBLISHING GROUP, INC.
NEW YORK

Published in 1988, 1992 by The Rosen Publishing Group, Inc.
29 East 21st Street, New York, New York 10010

Revised Edition, 1992
Copyright © 1988, 1992 by The Rosen Publishing Group, Inc.

Printed in Canada

Library of Congress Cataloging-in-Publication Data

Ball, Jacqueline A.
    Everything you need to know about drug abuse / Jacqueline A. Ball
(The Need to know library)
    Bibliography: p. 62
    Includes index.
    Summary: Describes a variety of drugs, from heroin and cocaine to
alcohol and caffeine, and examines their abuse and what can be done to
prevent it.
    ISBN 0-8239-1402-X
    1. Drug abuse—United States—Juvenile literature. 2. Teenagers—
United States—Drug use—Juvenile literature. 3. Drug abuse—United
States—Prevention—Juvenile literature. [1. Drugs. 2. Drug abuse.]
I. Title. II. Series.
HV5828.B34   1988
362.2'9—dc19   88–15651
                                                                      CIP
                                                                       AC

Contents

Introduction

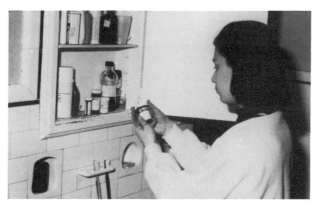

Sometimes drug abuse starts with pills from the medicine chest.

Every year more than *a half-million* people go to the hospital with diseases caused by alcohol. One out of every six deaths in America last year was caused by smoking. Each day nearly 5,000 people try cocaine for the first time—even though cocaine can kill you the first time you use it.

Why? Why do people abuse drugs that can cause so much harm? There are many reasons. You may have felt some of them yourself.

○ Pressure to go along with the crowd.
○ Poor self-esteem. You hope drugs will make you feel like a better person.
○ You have too many problems at home, at school, with friends. You need a way out.
○ You want to take a risk, have a thrill.

Drug takers soon find that they can't perform well, at school, on the job, or at home. Adults become unable to support themselves and their families. They use all their money to buy drugs. This scares them, so they take more drugs.

Drug abusers can be any age. Many older people take drugs to help them sleep. Or they use drugs to feel calm. Then they need other drugs. It is hard to wake up. Or they don't have much energy.

Every part of a person's life can be harmed by drug abuse. A person's mind can be harmed. Body organs like the heart and lungs can be hurt, too.

One of the worst kinds of harm comes from *addiction*. Addiction means falling into a habit. It can happen after days or weeks of using certain drugs. The drug becomes part of your body's chemistry. Your body needs more and more of the drug. It can no longer work without it.

Not all drugs are addictive to your body. But all drugs can be addictive to your mind. You get into a habit. You like the feeling you get when you smoke or drink or take pills. You don't want to be without that feeling. So you take more. Soon your life is centered around this drug.

This book will not just tell you how drugs hurt. It will also tell you where to get help. You will find out where to turn if you or someone you know needs help with a drug problem.

All drugs and medicines should be used with care. It is important to
follow directions.

Chapter 1

What Is A Drug?

You've heard of drugs. You've also heard that they are bad for you. But you take medicines when you're sick. Aren't medicines drugs? Are all medicines bad for you? What is the difference between drugs and medicines?

Use vs. Abuse

James is sick. He has a high fever and coughs. The doctor gives him a drug. Soon he is feeling well again.

Sharon is depressed. She is failing history. Her boyfriend doesn't call. A friend suggests she smoke some pot. For a while Sharon feels great. Then she's just as depressed as before.

What's the difference? James took a legal drug to cure an illness. The doctor who prescribed the drug knew what it would do to James.

Sharon took an illegal drug to forget her problems. She hoped it would make her feel good. But she did not really know what the drug might do.

Most medicines are taken for only a short time. Drugs like marijuana and heroin are just the opposite. The more people take, the more they want.

So medicines *are* drugs, but they are drugs we need. We use them to help us get well and stay well. When taken as directed they do not harm us.

Some drugs are not medicines. Drugs like alcohol, marijuana, cocaine, heroin, amphetamines, and barbiturates are called *abused* drugs. You may know them as booze, pot, coke, crack, horse, speed, or uppers and downers. By any name, these drugs harm the body. They are not healing medicines.

Protecting Your Health

"Take only as directed by a doctor." You hear these words on TV and radio ads. Even legal drugs can be harmful if abused.

Nina's grandmother takes valium for depression. A doctor wrote the prescription for her valium. The pills sit in plain sight on her Grandmother's bathroom shelf.

"Try some," Nina's friends tell her. "They'll make you real laid back." But Nina is scared. She doesn't know what the valium might do to her. And she doesn't want to find out.

It is dangerous to mix different drugs and to mix drugs and alcohol.

A healthy mind and body are precious gifts. But the chemicals in drugs can damage the billions of cells in the body. The cells in the brain and nervous system are hurt the most. This damage leads to mental, physical, and emotional problems. Some of the problems can have fearful effects. A young man who used Methedrine ("speed") says:

"...when you're shooting speed you start to feel like there's bugs going around under your skin and you know they're not there but you pick at them anyway. I'm always trying to pick them out of my eyebrows."

Speed freaks also often feel that someone is after them. They get angry at ordinary remarks. This feeling is called paranoia. It can lead to murder or suicide.

This kind of anger can lead to child abuse, too. Some parents drink too much alcohol. Or they take other dangerous drugs. They can lose all judgment and control. Sometimes they take out their problems on their children. They beat them or hurt them in other ways. Many abused children then grow up to be abusive parents.

Drugs and the Law

If drugs are bad, why do they *sound* so good? The harm of drug abuse is hidden. People use fun terms like "getting high" when they talk about drugs. These words trick people. They make people think drugs are harmless. They make taking drugs sound like a way to have fun. People forget that taking drugs can hurt their bodies and minds.

You might forget something else, too. *Most harmful drugs are illegal.* It is against the law to buy, sell, or use drugs. If you do so and you are discovered, you will be punished under the law. *That* is the truth.

Summary
○ Medicines are not harmful when taken as directed.
○ Drugs like marijuana are not medicines.
○ They are called *abused* drugs.
○ The chemicals in abused drugs damage the body's cells.
○ The damage leads to mental, physical, and emotional problems.
○ Most harmful drugs are illegal.

Chapter 2

Heroin

Heroin is also known as "junk," "smack," and "horse." Heroin is a narcotic. A narcotic is a powerful drug. It takes away pain and makes you sleep.

One of the first narcotics was opium. Opium comes from the poppy flower. Later, doctors made another drug from opium, called morphine. Both saved lives in surgery. They eased the pain of men wounded on the battlefield.

Doctors discovered that morphine was very addictive. They created heroin to solve this problem. Heroin comes from morphine.

Doctors quickly found that heroin was even more addictive than morphine. They stopped using it. But it was too late. Criminals had already discovered it.

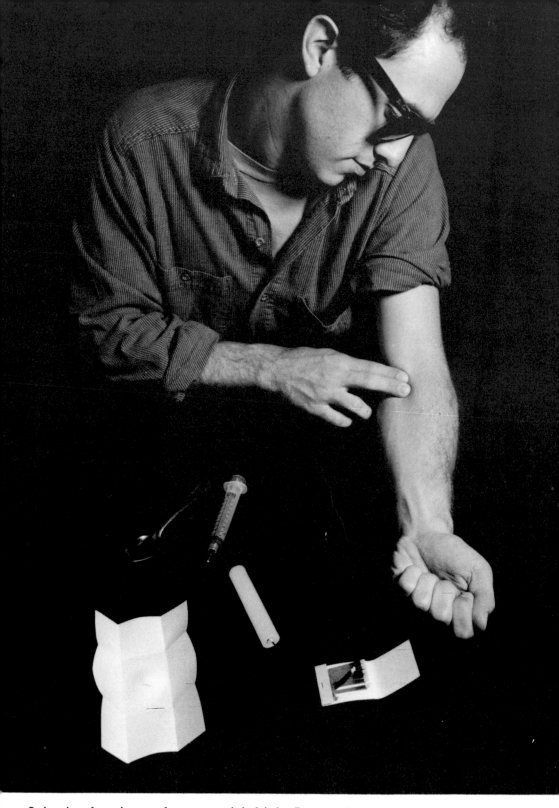

Injecting heroin produces a quick high. It can also cause sudden death.

Heroin is a terrible drug. It produces a powerful high. But the dangers are not worth it. First, it slows down breathing and heartbeat. If one of these actually stops, it means death. Other serious dangers can result from heroin use.

To get the effects of heroin quickly, users inject it. "Skin-popping" is injecting the drug just under the skin. This way it gets into the bloodstream through tiny blood vessels. Another kind of injection, called "mainlining," is more dangerous. When addicts mainline, they inject heroin directly into a vein. The effects of the drug are felt very quickly.

Addicts give themselves injections daily, often several times a day. The skin of their arms and legs is often covered with needle sores, called "tracks." These sores can get infected and ooze.

Constant injections can result in other health dangers. Hepatitis, a serious blood disease, is common among drug addicts. An even worse threat is AIDS, acquired immune deficiency syndrome. This disease is carried in the blood and can be passed from one addict to another when needles are shared. AIDS is fatal. If you get AIDS, you will die. Doctors have not yet found a cure.

Heroin has other dangers, too:

Heroin damages the eyes. It keeps the pupils dilated so that the eyes are very sensitive to light. Heroin addicts wear dark glasses, even at night.

Heroin stops *all* the body cells from working properly. They can't get the nutrition they need to stay healthy.

Your body can't hold onto calcium. Your teeth rot, and your bones break.

Addicts stop caring about how they look. They forget to wash. Many junkies have lice.

You stop caring about anything except having enough of the drug. It is hard to work, or stay in school.

Crime and violence are common among heroin addicts. Illegal drugs are very expensive. And addicts will do *anything* to get money to buy drugs.

Because heroin is so addictive, it is easy to overdose. You just keep taking more and more. If you inject more heroin than your body can handle, you will die.

Summary

○ Heroin is in the opium family.
○ It is extremely addictive.
○ It takes over every cell of your body. It makes your teeth rot. Bones break easily. Vision is damaged.
○ Heroin addicts are likely to commit crimes for drug money.
○ Death from overdose is always near.

Chapter 3

Cocaine and Crack

The ballet star is in her dressing room. People praise her talent all over the world. She is brilliant and beautiful. She has everything—including a habit. Before she goes onstage, she sprinkles some white powder on the glass of her dressing table. Then she takes a straw and inhales the powder.

The young athlete is talking to the press. He has just signed a contract with the Boston Celtics. His mother wipes away a proud tear as she looks at her handsome son. There is a party later. Everyone surrounds him, wanting to be his friend. One "friend" gives him some white powder. The athlete thinks, "Just once can't hurt." Days later his mother is wiping away tears of sorrow.

These are real people. The ballerina is Gelsey Kirkland. She ruined her life, health, and career with cocaine.

The basketball star was Len Bias. He went one step further. He died from cocaine, possibly the first time he tried it.

Cocaine is an odorless powder that is sometimes white as snow. Some people even call it "snow." Pure "coke" is so deadly that a one-gram dose will kill you. It takes only a tiny bit to make you high.

Cocaine is called a narcotic. But it is not like other narcotics. It does not cause sleep or kill pain.

Cocaine stimulates you. It makes you feel great, able to do anything. It puts you into a state of *euphoria*. You feel happy, hopeful, on top of the world. But the feeling doesn't last long.

Most people "snort" cocaine. Snorting is inhaling powder through your nose. It passes through the mucous membranes in your nose into the bloodstream. Then it works on the nervous system. Your blood pressure goes up, and you breathe faster.

Next it works on the brain. It makes you think you can do *anything*. Some people even claim that their muscles are stronger when they use coke. (Scientists say they are imagining things.)

Continued use of coke is dangerous. Your nose can collapse. You become very nervous and

Len Bias's great career as a basketball star ended suddenly.
He died from cocaine.

sensitive to noise. As brain cells die, you lose your memory. You can suffer from hallucinations. You may think people are out to get you. You cannot control yourself. You can end up killing somebody over something unimportant.

Cocaine can cause a heart attack. That's what killed Len Bias. The coke interfered with his heartbeat.

Cocaine can do all these terrible things. But it is not addictive. Your body does not develop a tolerance for it. But your mind craves it. You want cocaine all the time. It takes control of your life. Ballerina Gelsey Kirkland said that using cocaine was like having another person living inside her. The "other person" made her do things to get cocaine.

She missed rehearsals. She ruined her performances. She roamed around the worst slums of New York, making drug deals. She had a bad cocaine dependence. She would do anything to get cocaine.

Some people get *too* high from coke. They can't stand the excitement. So they take a sedative to calm down. Coke mixed with heroin is used this way. It's called a "speedball." Comedian John Belushi was "shooting" (injecting) a speedball when he died.

Some people would rather smoke coke than snort it. They treat it with ether. Then they heat it with a torch. This is known as "freebasing." The comedian Richard Pryor was freebasing and the ether exploded. He was badly burned.

There's nothing funny about cocaine. Richard Pryor would tell you that himself. So would John Belushi—if he could.

Crack

The number one drug on the streets today is *crack*. Thousands of addicts are trying to kick the habit. Thousands more are on waiting lists for treatment centers.

Crack is three-quarters cocaine. Unlike cocaine, crack *is* addictive. Police say it is responsible for countless violent crimes. Crack takes just seconds to get to your brain. The high lasts only a few minutes. When the rush stops, the crash begins.

Freebasing cocaine.

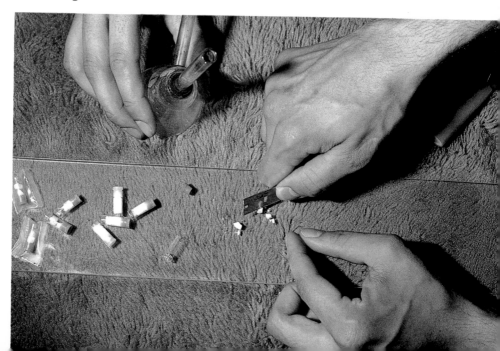

Snorting cocaine has many harmful effects.

Down you go, losing energy, out of control, hating yourself. The minute you come down, you want to go up again. So you go out looking for more crack. And you get it any way you can.

Take a look at exactly what crack does to your body:

Skin: It makes your skin oily. It turns your skin ugly gray or yellow.

Blood vessels: It makes the blood race through your veins so hard that they can actually burst.

Eyes: It causes oversensitivity to light. You begin to see little halos around things.

Heart: It changes the normal rhythm of your heartbeat. It makes your heart skip beats. Even if you're a teenager, crack can make you have a heart attack.

Lungs: Crack makes the tubes leading to your lungs fill up with mucus. You get a constant cough. You can get pneumonia.

Muscles: It overstimulates your muscles and makes them cramp.

Behavior, emotions: Crack breaks your concentration. It pushes you up high and then pulls you way down. It can lead to crimes such as drug dealing, stealing, and prostitution.

If you know someone who is using crack, *get help.* Crack addiction can be treated. A cocaine habit is treatable, too. Call this number: 1-800-COCAINE, for advice on breaking free.

Summary
○ Cocaine is a narcotic. It gives you a rush of confidence and well-being.
○ It is *not* physically addicting, like heroin or amphetamines. Your tissues do not build a tolerance for it.
○ It *is* mentally addicting. People can't stay away from it.
○ Cocaine damages your brain. It harms all of your body organs and systems. It can cause even a very young person to have a heart attack and die.
○ Crack is a drug that is mostly cocaine. It is smoked instead of snorted.
○ Crack *is* physically addicting. Your tissues build a tolerance for it. Your body always needs more.

Chapter 4

Amphetamines

Jessica is fifteen. She is very pretty and popular. Her only problem is her weight. She thinks she's too fat. Jessica has a friend who is very overweight. She gives Jessica some pills she says she got from her doctor. Jessica takes the pills. She is delighted by the energy she suddenly has. Her appetite is totally gone. She hums and sings as she cleans her room. She does her hair and then irons her clothes. She washes the car and then takes a long walk.

After a couple of days, Jessica begins to get scared. She can feel her heart beating like crazy. She can't sleep a wink. Her mouth is dry, and she knows her breath is disgusting. What could be in those pills? A doctor prescribed them. How could they be bad?

Diet pills that contain amphetamines speed up the nervous system. A false sense of energy is the result of this kind of drug.

The pills Jessica is taking are called amphetamines. They were invented to treat diseases. Now they are used often for other reasons.

For years many doctors prescribed amphetamines for weight loss or lack of energy. But the pills were badly abused. Now the Federal Drug Administration (FDA) says amphetamines can only be prescribed for three medical problems. One is narcolepsy (a disease that makes people sleepy all the time). Another is hyperactivity, which makes children restless all the time. The third is extreme overweight.

Amphetamines speed up the nervous system. That is why they are called "speed," or "pep pills." All the cells in the body work faster. That means the muscles work faster. The brain and heart work harder. The blood circulates faster. Energy is drained from the cells at a very rapid rate. People who depend on amphetamines (Methadrine, Benzedrine, and others) are called "speed freaks." They cannot function without the drugs.

Usually, when the body runs out of energy the nervous system sends warning signals. Hunger is a warning signal. It means we need nourishment. Tiredness is a warning signal. It means we need to rest.

When people take amphetamines, those warning signals are shut off. They have no way to tell that it is time to eat or sleep. What happens?

People collapse. They can even die.

Scientists believe that abusing amphetamines can lead to addiction (being unable to stop using them). They think amphetamines can cause brain damage. They *know* that withdrawing from them is a nightmare. Users trying to kick the pep pill habit feel very tired. They have bad headaches and stomach pains. Muscles cramp, and sweat pours out. And these effects take a while to disappear. It can take longer to withdraw than it does to get hooked.

Summary

- Amphetamines are pills that speed up the nervous system.
- They are *addictive*. The more you take, the more you need to take to feel the effects.
- They shut off natural warning signs. People "forget" to eat or rest.
- People can collapse, and even die, from their effects.
- They can cause brain damage.
- Withdrawal from their use is painful and frightening.
- The government has strictly limited the use of amphetamines because they have been so badly abused.

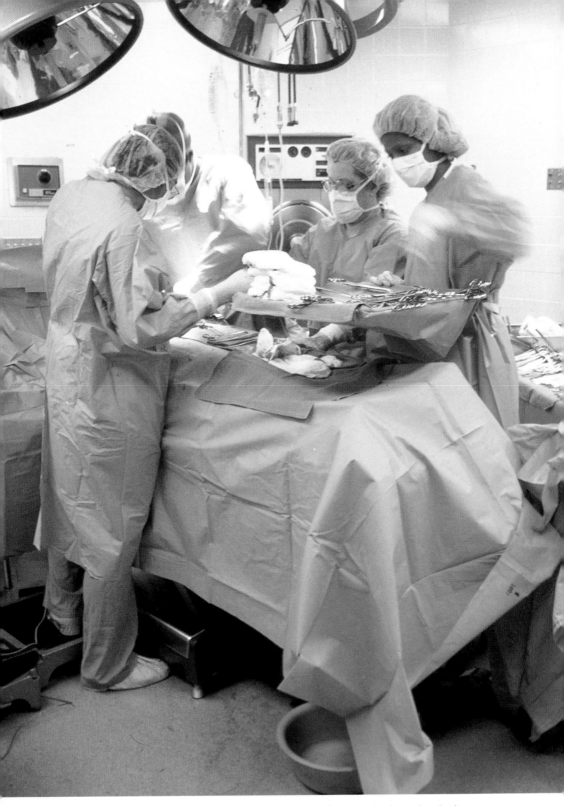

To help patients relax before surgery, they are given sedatives in their rooms. Anesthesia is given in the operating room.

Chapter 5

Barbiturates and Other Sedatives

Barbiturates are the opposite of amphetamines. These drugs depress the nervous system. They slow down the heartbeat, breathing, and blood pressure. Another name for barbiturates is sedatives. They're also called "downers."

Sedatives have real medical uses. They are used to help patients relax before surgery. They are also used to treat high blood pressure and ulcers. But too many people take them for other reasons. People take barbiturates because they are lonely or frustrated. They want to tune out their problems.

You can get drunk on barbiturates, just as you can on liquor. Your tissues develop a tolerance for them over time. This means that they are addictive. You need more and more to feel the effects. That is what happened to Jessica.

Remember Jessica, from the last chapter? She was taking amphetamines to lose weight. But they gave her so much energy that she couldn't sleep.

She wanted to keep losing weight. So she didn't want to stop taking the amphetamines. She went to the drugstore and bought some sleeping pills, but they didn't work.

Then she remembered something. Last year her mother had been having sleepless nights. It was about the time her father had made a job change. Mom went to the doctor. Maybe he gave her some . . . yes! Jessica found the bottle of pills in her parents' bathroom. Seconal, the label said. There were still plenty left.

After that, life was great. Take an upper in the morning. Run around all day, losing weight the whole time. Take a "seccy" at night. Sleep like a baby.

Until Jessica began to feel tense all the time. She would start crying or laughing suddenly. Friends told her she wasn't acting like herself.

Soon one pep pill couldn't wake her up enough. She started taking two. Then one seccy couldn't put her to sleep. She started taking more of those.

She ran out of Seconals. She lost control of herself. Her parents heard her screaming. She was jumping on her bed, tearing down the curtains. They got her to a clinic just in time. Now Jessica is under a doctor's care. She is going through painful barbiturate withdrawal. Withdrawal is the process your body goes through when you stop taking drugs.

Jessica was caught in a cycle called dualism, the use of two opposite drugs. She took one pill to speed her up. She took another to slow her down. She went up, down, up, down, on a deadly seesaw. Combining drugs like this has caused many deaths.

A very dangerous combination is alcohol and barbiturates. This mixture depresses the involuntary brain centers. Those centers control the automatic actions your body makes, like the beating of your heart and breathing. It can depress them so badly that they stop.

Tranquilizers

You may know tranquilizers by names like Librium and Valium. Tranquilizers are very much like barbiturates. Here is a list of symptoms. They are caused by the abuse of tranquilizers or barbiturates.

○ Thick speech
○ Blurred vision
○ Mixed up words and thoughts
○ Lack of energy
○ Slow reactions

Use of tranquilizers or barbiturates can lead to abuse. Abuse can lead to overdose. Overdose leads to death.

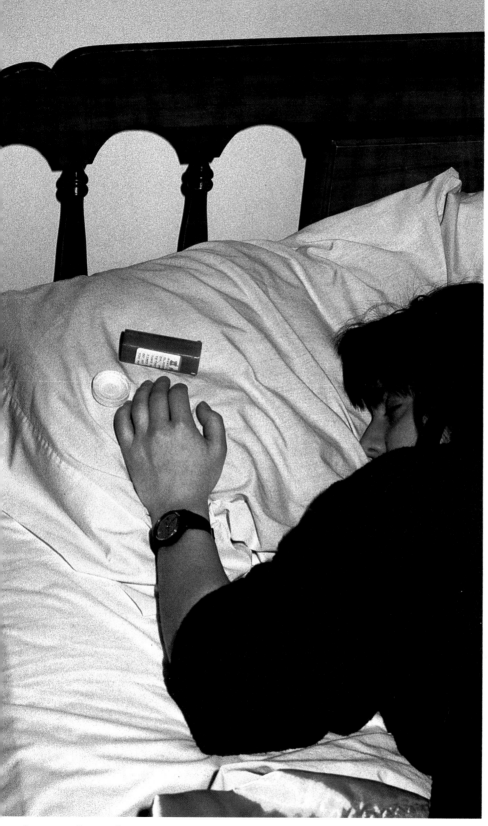

An overdose of tranquilizers can lead to death.

Quaaludes

The sedative known as Quaalude is a dangerous drug. Its real name is *methaqualone*.

In only one year Quaaludes caused the death of more than 300 people. More than fifty of those people committed suicide. Why? Quaaludes can cause horrible hallucinations. You might say these people were *scared to death*. They saw dreadful things on Quaalude trips that made them want to die.

Even *stopping* this drug can kill you. Withdrawal must be done under a doctor's care. Otherwise you can die from severe ulcers, sores that cause bleeding in your stomach. Or your lungs will fail and you will die.

Summary

○ Barbiturates are the opposite of amphetamines.
○ Barbiturates depress the involuntary brain centers that control heartbeat and breathing.
○ They are addictive. Your body's tissues develop a tolerance for them. The more you take, the more you need.
○ Some users combine barbiturates with other drugs. This combination is called dualism. It can result in death.
○ Tranquilizers have the same effects on your body as barbiturates do.

Terrible fear can be caused by some drugs. A person may hear and see things that are not there.

Chapter **6**

Mind-Changing Drugs and Hallucinogens

*A*nne couldn't believe her good luck. Joey had gotten tickets to the concert. He had also gotten some mescaline. Anne had "dropped" mescaline before. She knew the music would be great while she was "tripping." At the last concert she felt like she was playing one of the guitars. Joey had thought he was a guitar! After the concert they had gone for ice cream. Each spoonful had seemed like an explosion of peach petals in Anne's mouth. They ate three pints.

But this time when they got to the concert, Anne knew something was different. Suddenly it seemed like the room was filled with boa constrictors who were trying to crush her. She started to scream and cry. Joey tried to lead her out but he couldn't find the door. Now he was scared, too.

Hallucinogenic Drugs

Mescaline and LSD are two drugs that cause hallucinations. They can make you see or hear things that are not there.

LSD is a colorless, odorless, and tasteless chemical. It is also called "acid." LSD looks like water, but it is a dangerous drug. A drop so small that you can't see it with a magnifying glass can cause hallucinations.

A hallucination under LSD or other drugs is sometimes called a "trip." When you are on a trip your senses get mixed up. You think you can "hear" colors. You seem to "see" sounds.
You can have a good trip like Anne and Joey did at the first concert. Or you can have a bad trip like Anne did the second time. *You can never tell in advance what kind of a trip it will be.*

LSD can drive a person insane. It damages the brain. It stops the normal activity of the brain cells. It gets into the message channels that connect the brain with the nervous system. Then the nerve cells get the wrong information.

Acid stays in your body a long time. You can have a flashback months after you stop taking the drug.

You cannot tell in advance when you're going to have a flashback. You cannot tell what the flashback is going to be like. You might feel spaced out, and confused.

Smoking marijuana can be harmful to the body. It may also cause brain damage.

Marijuana, Hashish, and THC

Not all mind-changing drugs cause hallucinations. Marijuana, often called "pot," relaxes people who smoke or eat it. Colors and sounds seem more intense. It makes some people very hungry. Others say they feel closer to people when they smoke pot.

Hashish is a concentrated form of marijuana. Its effects are like pot only stronger. Hash is usually smoked with a special pipe. Marijuana is a dried weed rolled into cigarettes called "joints."

Often people who smoke pot or hash lose track of time. Minutes seem like hours. It is very dangerous to drive when your sense of time is so changed. People who have used pot or hash may have very red eyes. They may not remember even basic facts. Their coordination may be off.

How can marijuana do these things? It contains a chemical with a dangerous power. The name of the chemical is *tetrahydrocannabinol*. Part of the name comes from the name of the marijuana plant, *Cannabis*. Most people use the short name of the chemical, THC. THC is released when the marijuana is smoked. THC enters the bloodstream through the lungs. The blood takes it to the brain, where it causes the high.

THC travels through your body fast. But it does not leave fast. THC stays in your blood three days. It stays in your lungs and liver at least a week. And it can remain in your brain a month.

THC is a danger to all body systems. It keeps your body's cells from taking in the right amount of protein. Your body does not get what it needs. It cannot stay healthy or fight off disease.

THC hurts your lungs. Doctors say that smoking five joints a week causes lung damage. It is as bad as smoking more than 100 regular cigarettes.

THC also harms your brain. Smoking pot dulls your mind by killing brain cells. If you smoke pot long enough you can suffer permanent brain damage. It can be harmful to smoke pot for even a short time. You will be tired all the time. You will be less interested in school.

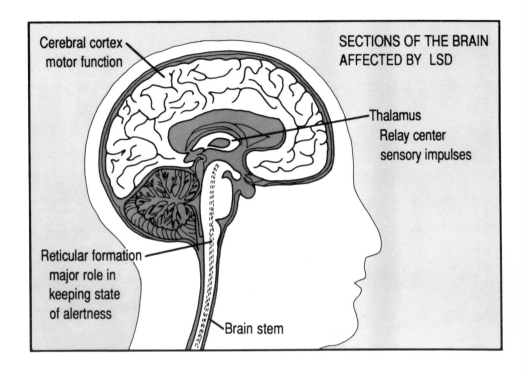

Cerebral cortex
motor function

SECTIONS OF THE BRAIN
AFFECTED BY LSD

Thalamus
Relay center
sensory impulses

Reticular formation
major role in
keeping state
of alertness

Brain stem

PCP: Terror Trip

Marijuana is bad, but *phencyclidine* is worse. The short name of this drug is PCP. But most people call it "angel dust." It is a hallucinogenic drug.

People swallow PCP in capsules. They sprinkle it on tobacco and smoke it. They dissolve it in liquid and inject it. But any way they use it, it is a drug with horrifying effects. It works mostly on the brain. It makes people act insane. Just listen to a teenager named Peter:

"Things happen every time I trip out. Once a hamburger looked like it was alive, and bleeding. Once I felt like snakes were crawling all over me."

One day Peter killed himself by accident. He was tripping, and he thought he could fly. He jumped off a building.

39

PCP stays in the brain for a long time. It stays in the body organs, too, such as the liver. That's why PCP users often experience a flashback. The drug suddenly takes effect again *even if they haven't touched it in months*.

Summary
○ Marijuana (pot), hashish (hash), PCP (angel dust), mescaline, and LSD (acid) are mind-changing drugs. They work through the brain. They can damage or kill brain cells.

○ PCP, LSD, and mescaline are hallucinogens. They mix up your senses and cause hallucinations. You may see or hear things that aren't really there.

○ These drugs work through the brain. They damage and kill brain cells.

○ These drugs stay in the body a long time. Users can have flashbacks months after they stop taking the drug.

○ Under the influence of these drugs users can hurt or even kill themselves or others.

○ You never know what will happen to you under the influence of the drug or what kind of trip you will have.

Chapter 7

Sniffing Glue and Other Things

"*What on earth could be the matter?*" *thought Mrs. Parson. She looked down at her student, Frank Roberts. He sat hunched over his desk, almost asleep. His nose was always running. He looked terrible. His behavior was terrible, too. He blew up for no reason.*

Mrs. Parson felt sorry for Frank. She had heard that his father and mother drank. Maybe they mistreated their children when they were drunk. She leaned down and gently touched Frank on the shoulder. He sprang away from her. She saw an ugly trail of scabs running from the back of Frank's hand up his arm. It looked as if he had been stabbed with a knife, again and again.

41

Mrs. Parson will soon find out what Frank's problem is. He is a glue sniffer. And he needs help.

Teenagers with problems at home are most likely to start sniffing glue. Or they may abuse other chemical substances. The chemicals give users a rush of heat and excitement. Those feelings make them forget their problems. Actually, the chemicals make them "drunk."

When they are drunk, they get violent. They often hurt themselves. Take the marks on Frank's arm, for instance. They *were* made by a knife. Frank used a knife to stab himself.

Glue sniffers hurt their bodies in other ways, too. Glue sniffers can die from suffocation. The chemicals can destroy their heart and lungs. Or they move on to harder drugs, such as heroin.

Glue isn't the only thing that people sniff. Anyone can buy "poppers" on the street. Poppers are bottles containing amyl nitrate or butyl nitrate.

These chemicals are legal. Glue is legal. But these substances *were not* created to be sniffed. They weren't invented to make people sick.

Summary

○ Sniffing glue, or any chemical, is dangerous.

○ Sniffing glue can lead to the use of harder drugs.

○ Sniffing glue often leads to violent acts against yourself.

Chapter 8

Alcohol: America's Most Abused Drug

Alcoholism among young people is increasing. That's why many states have raised the minimum drinking age to twenty-one. Even so, kids say they're feeling pressured to drink earlier and earlier. A third of American fourth graders said in a poll that their friends pressure them to drink.

The Figures Are Frightening

○ One out of five American teenagers has a drinking problem.
○ More than 3 million young Americans are in trouble with alcohol.
○ Driving and drinking kills more than 3,600 American teens a year. Nearly 85,000 a year are hurt.

43

Alcohol acts on the brain. The brain may send mixed-up messages, and cause slurred speech and staggering.

○ Half of the murders in the U.S. and a third of the suicides have some connection with alcohol.

Who Is an Alcoholic?

Alcoholism is a disease. It affects people who are addicted to alcohol. Alcoholics cannot control their need to drink.

Five million Americans abuse alcohol. You might never realize that they are alcohol abusers. These people don't look or act like bums. They look normal. They lead respectable lives. And they are of every age. Even grade-school children are abusing alcohol. And the problem has reached shocking proportions among teenagers. Bonnie G. is an example.

Bonnie is 15. She has been drinking since she was 10. Every morning she carries a canteen of wine to school. She says it helps her get through the day. Teachers don't bother her when she's in her wine-soaked glow. Bonnie's parents don't know that she drinks—or they don't want to know it.

How Alcohol Affects Your Body

Isn't it safer to drink beer or wine than liquor? No! All three drinks are dangerous. The alcohol in a 12 oz. mug of beer is about the same as in a 5 oz. wine glass or in 1½ oz. shot glass of liquor.

Alcohol is a clear, colorless liquid. The alcohol in beer, wine, or liquor is made from grains. There is more alcohol in a smaller amount of liquor than there is in a small amount of beer or wine. But all three kinds of drinks can cause great damage.

Alcohol causes the brain to send mixed up messages to the body. You may slur your speech or stagger when you walk. You may get angry or violent without reason. The next day you might have a hangover: upset stomach, headache, trouble thinking clearly.

Alcohol Kills

Many other parts of your body are affected by alcohol. Alcohol makes blood vessels expand. More blood travels out to the small vessels under the skin. That means that your body is losing heat. People just *think* alcohol warms them up. Really, the opposite is happening. Alcoholics who wander the streets in winter can freeze to death.

The liver is the organ that is most affected by alcohol. One job of the liver is to filter alcohol out of the blood. The liver also helps the body get rid of it. *But the liver can only handle one quarter of an ounce of alcohol per hour.* That is only part of the alcohol in one glass of wine, or a beer, or a mixed drink. If you drink more than that, the liver works harder. Liver cells turn fatty, then hard as a rock. Heavy drinking for a long time can cause cirrhosis of the liver. Cirrhosis is a fatal disease.

Alcohol has been linked to cancer of the stomach, mouth, and throat. It can also damage your kidneys. Drinking liquor—even a little bit—while pregnant can cause birth defects.

One of the worst things about alcohol is what can happen when people drive drunk. The National Safety Council says that one out of every fifty drivers is driving drunk. Liquor causes more than half of all fatal motor vehicle accidents.

Just Say "No"

It's hard to say "no" to friends. Try one of these reasons along with your "no."
- "I've seen alcohol wreck too many people's lives. I don't want it wrecking mine."
- "I can have more fun without drinking."
- Maybe you drive a car, have a job, play a sport, or belong to a group that does not allow drinking. Those are great reasons to say "no."

Summary
- Alcohol is a legal drug. It is abused by millions of Americans.
- Alcoholism is a disease.
- Heavy drinking hurts body organs and brain cells.
- Drunk driving accounts for half of all highway deaths.

The nicotine in cigarettes is a poison.

Chapter 9

Tobacco

> ## WARNING: Tobacco Products Are Hazardous to Your Health

Smoking means death. How? Why? Because each of the 580 billion cigarettes produced every year is full of poison. Each puff of smoke brings *carbon monoxide, cyanide, ammonia sulfide.*

Tars and Nicotine

Of course, each drag brings you nicotine, too. In large amounts, nicotine is also a poison. If you got enough of it in your blood, you would suffocate. Its powerful poison would paralyze the muscles of your lungs and chest.

Even in tiny doses, nicotine is bad news. It is addicting and harmful. It makes your nerves shaky and unsteady. It speeds up your heartbeat. It raises

your blood pressure. It harms your digestive system.
When a pregnant woman smokes, her baby may
not weigh as much as it should when it is born.

Cancer, Emphysema, and Heart Disease

Besides nicotine and poisonous gases, each
cigarette you smoke contains poisonous solids, too.
These are called *tars*. Specks of these tars stick to
the inside of your lungs.

Soon your lungs are thickly coated with them.
The coating turns black. It blocks the air sacs
in your lungs.

The next stage is cancer. Abnormal cells grow in
the lungs. The growth is stimulated by the cancer-
causing substances in cigarettes—nicotine, tars, and
poisonous gases.

There is no such thing as a safe cigarette. Filtered
cigarettes have *more* tars and nicotine than
unfiltered ones. (The tars and nicotine produce the
taste.) King-sized cigarettes may reduce tars and
nicotines *if* you smoke only half of them. But you
are still getting some poisons.

You can get a constant cough. You can develop
bronchitis. You can get a lung disease called
emphysema. People with severe emphysema need
to wheel around a little cart of oxygen wherever
they go. Without the oxygen, they cannot breathe.

If you smoke, you can develop heart disease. Smoking makes your blood vessels tighten up. They cannot relax. Blood can stay too long in one place. When that happens, a blood clot can form. The clot is a thick mass of blood.

A blood clot is dangerous. It can break away from the spot where it forms and travel to some other part of your body. If it goes to your brain it will cause a stroke.

Other Tobacco Products

Cigarettes are not the only form of tobacco that can be dangerous. Cigar and pipe smokers get cancer of the mouth, throat, or lips.

Chewing tobacco is not as dry as cigarette or pipe tobacco. A user puts a small wad of it into the mouth. Chewing tobacco spares the lungs, but it can do much damage to the mouth and stomach. Another tobacco taken through the mouth is snuff. It is placed between the cheek and the gum line. In the old days people used to sniff it. This caused damage to the nose as well.

Summary
o Smoking brings death. Smokers have a much higher early death rate than nonsmokers.
o One million of today's teenagers will die from lung cancer as adults.
o Nicotine is addicting. The more cigarettes you smoke, the more you need.

Coffee and soda can perk you up temporarily. The caffeine stimulates the brain, but it is not real energy.

Chapter 10

The Perk-Me-Ups

How do you start your day? A cup of coffee or tea? A can of Pepsi or Coke? A bowl of chocolate coated cereal? If so, you're using caffeine to get you going.

What Harm Can Caffeine Do?

Caffeine is a drug. Foods made from cola nuts, cocoa beans, coffee beans, or tea leaves contain caffeine. Caffeine perks you up by exciting the brain and nervous system.

But caffeine can do a lot of damage. It is a high price for a quick pick-me-up. It can also cause headaches, diarrhea, irregular heartbeat, and ringing in the ears. Caffeine can make it hard to get to sleep. Inability to sleep is called *insomnia*. Caffeine can make you depressed, cranky, short-tempered and overly concerned about yourself.

Cutting Down on Caffeine

No one should have more than 200 milligrams (mg.) of caffeine a day. Just one cup of coffee has half that amount or more. Tea has about 65 mg. of caffeine per cup. A non-cola soft drink can have as much caffeine as a cola drink, from 30–70 mg. in a 12 oz. can. Many cold medicines are also high in caffeine. Pills that help you stay awake or help keep your appetite down are very high in caffeine. One of these pills alone can have up to 200 mg. of caffeine.

How can you break the caffeine habit? If you drink a lot of soda, buy only the decaffeinated kinds. Or have a glass of juice instead. If you must drink coffee or tea, use decaffeinated brands or herbal teas. Carob is a good substitute for chocolate. Better yet, try hard candy. It has no chocolate, and therefore no caffeine.

Summary

○ Caffeine is a drug. It can be habit forming.
○ It stimulates the central nervous system. It affects a person's systems and moods.
○ No one should consume more than 200 milligrams of caffeine a day.

Chapter 11

Just Say "No" to Drugs

You've seen this advice on posters, on T-shirts, on TV. But sometimes saying "No" can be much harder than it sounds. One good way to avoid saying "No" is to avoid people who use drugs. Choose friends who don't smoke or drink or do drugs. If you're not around drugs, you won't have to say "No"!

It Won't Happen to Me

Jana knew how drugs could wreck a family. Her father had a cocaine habit. He spent every cent he made on cocaine. Her mother had to get a second job just to feed her family. Now they were getting divorced. Yet Jana smoked pot with her friends almost every day. "Pot's different," she told herself. "And besides, I'd never let myself get hooked like my dad did."

Jana may *think* she can control a drug habit. But she's wrong. Different drugs affect different people in different ways. You never know how you will be affected. It could be different each time you take the drug. All drugs have some effect on the body and mind. And those effects are *never* good.

The best way—the *easiest* way—is *never to let them in*. Does that mean you can never have a beer? Well, you can't until you're of legal age. But after that, no, it doesn't mean you can never have a beer. Your body can handle an occasional drink if *you* can handle moderation.

But moderation is *not* the answer for other drugs. *The only way to handle most drugs is total abstinence, total avoidance.*

D.A.R.E.

Drug Abuse Resistance Education is a program to help keep kids off drugs. You may have a D.A.R.E. program in your school. A local police officer and a teacher work together to help kids. How can D.A.R.E. help you?
○ It teaches you about the use and abuse of drugs.
○ It teaches you how to stand up to pressure from friends and gangs so you can say "No."
○ It teaches you how to be proud of yourself.
○ It shows you how to handle stress without taking drugs.

Chapter 12

When It's Time to Get Help

If someone you know has a drug problem, be a friend. Show support for the person. But do not support the person's drug use. Ask your friend to get help from an adult, the school, or a counseling center.

If your friend won't get help, then you must step in. Tell an adult *you* trust. Don't think of it as letting your friend down. Think of it as being a friend. Think of it as maybe saving your friend's life.

To get help, look in the phone book yellow pages under "Alcoholism" or "Drug Abuse." Check the pages called "Community Services." You won't have to give your name when you call.

One *very important* last thing. If there is a medical emergency, such as an overdose, *get help fast!* Dial "O" for Operator. Or dial 911, or the emergency number in your town. Tell the person who answers exactly what happened. Describe the victim's symptoms. Give the complete address.

Many organizations have groups around the country to help with drug abuse. If you can't find a local number in your phone book, call one of these main numbers. They can tell you where to call.

Alanon Family Group Headquarters
P.O. Box 182, Madison Square Station
New York, NY 10010
212-302-7240

Alcohol and Drug Problems Association
1101 15th Street NW
Washington, DC 20005
202-737-4340

National Clearinghouse for Drug Abuse Information: Provides information about all types of drugs. Write P.O. Box 1908; Rockville, MD 20850

Alcoholics Anonymous World Services
Box 459, Grand Central Station
New York, NY 10017
212-686-1100

Cocaine and Crack Hotline: 1-800-COCAINE

National Institute on Drug Abuse Treatment Referral: Tells you where to call to get the right kind of help for any kind of drug or alcohol problem. Call toll free: 1-800-622-HELP.

Glossary—*Explaining New Words*

addictive Causing physical dependency.

alcohol Intoxicating substance.

alcoholism A disease in which a person becomes addicted to alcohol.

amphetamine Artificial stimulant; substance that peps you up.

angel dust Slang name for PCP.

barbiturate Artificial depressant.

Benzedrine An amphetamine.

caffeine Mild stimulant found in coffee beans, tea leaves, kola nuts, and cocoa beans.

cell Small unit of a living thing; cells are specialized: brain cells, skin cells, blood cells, etc.

cocaine White, powdery drug, the effects of which include feelings of power and happiness.

coke Slang name for cocaine.

crack Cocaine in a form that can be smoked.

depressant Drug that depresses the brain, slows down brain activity.

drug dependency Inability to do without a particular drug.

dualism Dependence on two drugs, one either to increase or decrease the effects of the other.

euphoria Feeling of extreme happiness.

flashback Recurrence of effects of a drug trip weeks or months after taking the drug.

grass Slang name for marijuana; others are weed, pot, mary jane.

hallucination Seeing sights and hearing sounds that are not really there.

hallucinogen   Substance that causes hallucinations.

hashish   Strong drug in the marijuana family.

heroin   Extremely addictive drug made from morphine.

horse   Slang name for heroin.

hyperactive   Constantly active.

intoxicated   Drunk.

LSD   Shortened name for d-lysergic acid diethylamide, a powerful hallucinogen.

mainline   To inject drugs into the veins.

marijuana   Leaves of the hemp plant, smoked to get a high.

mescaline   A hallucinogenic drug made from a type of cactus.

Methedrine   An amphetamine.

morphine   Sleep-causing, pain-killing drug made from the opium poppy.

narcolepsy   Disease that brings on sudden attacks of deep sleep.

narcotics   A group of very addictive drugs, most made from the opium poppy, that help relieve pain and bring on sleep.

nicotine   Addictive substance in tobacco.

opium   Drug made from the opium poppy.

paranoia   Mental disorder that makes people think others are "out to get them."

phencyclidine (PCP)   Powerful drug that causes hallucinations.

psychedelic   Able to cause the wild colors and

patterns seen during hallucinations.

Quaalude Trade name for the sedative methaqualone.

Seconal Barbiturate, "downer," powerful sleeping pill.

sedative Drug that depresses the central nervous system, developed to help people to be calm or to sleep.

self-esteem How you feel about yourself.

skin-popping Injecting drugs under the skin.

snort To inhale drugs through the nose.

speed Slang name for amphetamine, especially for powerful forms of the drug.

speedball Injection of cocaine and heroin.

stimulant Drug that speeds up activities of the body's cells.

tetrahydrocannabinol (THC) Substance in marijuana that causes euphoria.

tranquilizer A calming drug. Valium and Librium are two common tranquilizers.

trip Experiences a person has after taking a hallucinogenic drug; changes in mental state and feelings.

ulcer Raw wound that bleeds easily, usually on the skin or in the stomach.

withdrawal Process of stopping the body's dependency on an addictive drug; physical and mental effects an addict suffers after ceasing to take an addictive drug.

For Further Reading

Fischman, F. "The Ups and Downs of Teen Drug Use." *Psychology Today*, February 1986, pages 68–69. (A) This article discusses the effects of drugs on young people.

Friedman, David (Consulting Editor). *Drug-Alert Series*. Frederick, MD: Twenty-First Century Books, 1990, 56–64 pages. A series of nine books, each dealing with a different group of drugs.

Madison, Arnold. *Drugs and You*, revised edition. New York: Messner, 1982, 80 pages. This book discusses the uses, abuses, and effects of various drugs, and the dangers of illegal drug use.

"Uppers are Really a Downer." *Current Health*, April 1987, pages 16–19. This article is about the dangers of amphetamine use.

Woods, Geraldine. *Drug Use and Drug Abuse*, Second edition. New York: Franklin Watts, 1986, 64 pages. A book discussing the uses of various drugs from hallucinogens to cough syrups.

Index

About the Author
Jacqueline A. Ball is the former editor of *Read,* a magazine for young adults focusing on the language arts. A former teacher, Ms. Ball was, until recently, executive editor of Juvenile Publishing at Field Publications, in Middletown, Connecticut. She now heads her own consultancy and product development firm.

About the Editor
Evan Stark is a well-known sociologist, educator, and therapist as well as a popular lecturer on women's and children's health issues. Dr. Stark was the Henry Rutgers Fellow at Rutgers University, an associate at the Institution for Social and Policy Studies at Yale University, and a Fulbright Fellow at the University of Essex. He is the author of many publications in the field of family relations and is the father of four children.

Acknowledgments and Photo Credits

P. 2, 6, 11, 25, 32, 34, 48, 52; p. 8, Stuart Rabinowitz; p. 14, Blackstar/Dan McCoy; p. 19, Wide World; p. 21, Blackstar/Joseph Rodriguez; p. 22, Sygma/A. Tannenbaum; p. 37, 44 Sygma/Louis Fernandez.

Design/Production: Blackbirch Graphics, Inc.
Cover Photograph: Stuart Rabinowitz